TIME SPACE AND DRUMS PART ONE

ROCK
DRUMMING
Foundation

ROCK
DRUMMING
Foundation

GRAVITY Volume 1 - Getting Grounded

The Time Space & Drums Series
A Complete Program of Lessons in Professional, Contemporary Rock and Jazz
Drumming Styles.

Written and Developed By:
Stephen Hawkins

Graphic Design By: Nathaniel Dasco.
Special Thanks To Linda Drouin and Ikhide Oshoma

ThinkeLife Publications

Stephen Hawkins – Time Space and Drums
Visit my website at www.timespaceanddrums.com

First printing: Jan 2018.

ISBN: 978 1 913929 00 8

Dedicated to the late Paul Daniels and family, Martin Daniels, Trevor Daniels, Paul Mellor's, Keith, Peter Windle, Andrew Marple's, Colin Keys, Peters & Lee, Susan Maughan, Ronnie Dukes, Tom O'Connor, Les Dennis, Bob Monkhouse, Bobby Davro, Tommy Bruce, Robert Young, Sandie Gold as well as the hundreds of other people who have played a part in my life experience. Including Sphinx Entertainment, E & B Productions as well as the hundreds of fantastic personalities I have had the pleasure of working alongside over the past 35 years. Apologies for anyone I have missed, not forgetting the current reader who I hope will receive as much from their drumming as I have and more – Stephen Hawkins.

Table of Contents

INTRODUCTION

In general, the top books in the drumming arena are more advanced drumming books aimed at solving a specific control issue or area of drumming: stick control, coordination, syncopation and such. Each of these title types is presented in a specific format for the drummer to practise. That format is more often than not lots of singular, one bar exercises crammed onto a single page.

But don't get me wrong, those types of books serve the drummer over many years mainly due to the number of variations covered. But when I think of those types of books, I always recall the now famous quote of Bruce Lee's that goes something like this: *"I fear not the man who has practiced 10,000 punches once, but I do fear the man who has practiced one punch 10,000 times."* It's plain to see what he meant when he spoke those immortal words. Paraphrased into the drumming practice arena, he was basically saying: Practise the fundamental exercises 10,000 times (and more, no limitation is implied) each rather than practicing 1000 exercises 10, 50, 100, 500, or 1000 times.

So, it doesn't really matter how well established a drummer, author or publisher is. The fact remains that less is more. Rather, less is much more. Put another way, many is mediocrity or even fantastic. But less is greatness! Or, it can be if you decide that it is.

So I urge you, whether you're a beginner just starting out on your drumming journey, an intermediate drummer wanting to further your current skills and make a name for yourself, or you're an advanced drummer looking for greatness, practise these exercises 10,000 times and more for no other reason than to build a powerful foundation for your future efforts. And remember, you cannot build a skyscraper on the foundations of a cottage or summer home. Unless of course your summer home is a skyscraper and you had already built the appropriate foundations.

For the beginner, this is about laying the foundations of your future drumming success. For the intermediate drummer, this is about laying the foundations for greater future drumming success. And for the advanced drummer, this is about disciplining yourself to improve even further by striving for greater perfection of the basic foundation. In short, this is all about self-discipline and seeking perfection and mastery. "It's not what you do, it's the way that you do it" holds true still.

It's not about learning the next sticking exercise or the next rudiment or the next anything that is achieved and then abandoned for the next shot of instant gratification. But as I suggested earlier, there is room for that also. Drumming should be fun, something you look forward to and there is no better feeling than playing something so basic yet realising that you played it ten times better today than you did yesterday. Others will notice that also.

So if you want to add a touch of finesse to your current level of skill and experience the transformation that goes along with practicing to the level of mastery, then it's time to start building a powerful foundation so you can later build your most magnificent structure as you grow and develop your skills further.

But for now, let's cover a few basic practice ideas and concepts. And, of course, for the beginner, I highly recommend Modern Drumming Concepts from this same series. For the most part, There are specific instructions that apply to every exercise you will find in the whole series. That is, play each one, two, or four-bar phrase through to the end of the bar and then repeat it once only. This is explained more in the Essence Email you will receive when you follow the link given later to download the audio demonstration file. Then, after you get used to stopping and starting the exercise, you should then repeat it while paying particular attention to the "how" you play it. Specifically, to play it scientifically and mathematically exact. Then, when you have done that for 1,000 hours (by that I mean a lot), it's then time to add technique to the equation to turn the scientifically exact exercise into a musical masterpiece. For now, technique is beyond this series of lessons. See the recommended section at the back of this book for more instruction on this.

So, just be content to practise these exercises with *precision* being the most vital element. Please note that 1,000 hours is 1 hour per day for 3 years. But I said earlier that this was fun. And so, when you first learn each exercise, practise them for as long as needed until you have mastered each lesson. This could be anything from 30 minutes to 30 days. Then...

1. When you can play each lesson and have spent one week just practising that lesson, go through the book until you have completed each lesson over a 6-week period. Spend 1 week on each lesson.
2. *Then, go through the book in 6 days by spending a whole day practising and striving for greater precision, one day per lesson. (If you are so inclined, you can spend 24 hours on each lesson; of course, that will take more than 1 day, practising 1 hour per day).*
3. Then, go through the whole book in 6 hours.
4. After which, you should go through the book, moving from one exercise to the next, all the time striving for greater precision as you play through the whole book in a single practise session.
5. You can then begin to add technique to the equation to further improve the feel

and flow of the exercises.

6. When you are at this point, you should begin your 10,000 hours.

In these earlier books 1 and 2... just play the exercises that include the fills and the basic complete beats. You can add other book in the series as you become familiar with each set of lessons. And go through the same 6-step process outlined above.

I have heard it said that the top drumming books, many of which were printed back in the 80s, are industry standards but my idea here is to specifically make complete mastery an industry standard. You achieve that when you begin to follow the 6 steps and begin the journey towards mastery. Remember that success is something you decide at the beginning; it is not a place you arrive or a journey. It is a choice you make at the beginning and therefore you begin to move *through success* which then breads more of the same.

The exercises and process covered in this series will absolutely make you a much better drummer with steady, demonstrable improvement along the way.

So, although other books may contain thousands of exercises that offer an endlessly challenging process through their various exercises and methods... The Time Space and Drum Series offers the same challenge but in a very different and more beneficial way. This is especially ideal for the beginning drummer. Instead of variety, our focus shifts to mastery, learning control of time, feel and dynamics as you learn the basics of reading and writing drum sheet music; it goes on to cover everything a beginner needs to know.

The fun part of drumming is then enhanced as you come to see leaps in progress because you disciplined yourself to stick with what truly matters. The foundations!

The beauty of this process or system is that although many won't learn anything new, almost every drummer will discover something about the most important part of drumming that often gets overlooked: the drummer. You will learn something about yourself as you go through this process even if it is, "I can't discipline myself to play this, it is boring" and so on. If something is boring, listen to a little Steve Gadd play some basic grooves. Great playing is anything but boring.

So, let's get down to the practicalities...

Drumming cannot, and should not, be divided into different categories or styles, although I have done so through this series. No matter how you interpret it, drumming is drumming. The drummer should, therefore, master all playing styles and situations. For example, think of any great rock drummers that you may know. After studying their background, you will usually find that he or she is a great Jazz drummer too. However, there is the odd exception.

The Time Space and Drums series doesn't divide the different styles. Instead, it integrates them. The combination of Jazz, Fusion, Funk, Punk, Heavy Metal and other music styles give the drummer an unbeatable edge, especially when backed by experience. It is those invaluable integrations and experiences that separate the average drummer from the great drummer. You should, of course, strive to become a great drummer.

Consider a drummer such as Neil Peart who plays for Rush (A Progressive Rock Style Band). When performing on The Buddy Rich Memorial Videos with the Buddy Rich Big Band, he played a basic jazz rhythm most of the way through the first tune. But he played it with POWER, CONTROL and a never swaying PRECISION. The power came from his vast experience as a progressive rock drummer. The control comes from his mastery of jazz and other techniques. However, when it was time for his drum solo, he blew the socks off the technicians. Some might think that he was uncomfortable in that situation, but the opposite is true. His playing, however, was very different from the millions of notes played by the other drummers. Neil Peart was a breath of fresh air.

The Time Space and Drums Series Files Are Like A Breath of Fresh Air!!!

Time Space and Drums Part 1 deals with 6 basic rhythms to be mastered by the student. These rhythms are split apart in order for you to perfect each limb one at a time. Then a basic drum-fill is used universally with the 6 rhythms to enable the drummer to perfect the flow of each rhythm. The idea being to create an image in the mind of the drummer of the whole rock drumming foundation, which will occur naturally over time.

During your study time, you should strive for a complete understanding of the theory as well as perfection as far as possible when practicing these rhythms, as they are the most widely used rhythms in drumming. If you're serious with your study, you should spare yourself nothing in order to perfect these basic rhythms. They are the foundation for everything else in drumming from a theoretical standpoint as well as a practical one.

These, along with the basic rhythms in Part 2, integrate the two aspects of modern drumming (Jazz & Rock) into one mighty tool or puzzle part. Parts 1 and 2 are the foundation you should strive to build in order to create a solid structure later through Parts 4-12 of the series.

Parts 1 and 2 are...

YOUR FOUNDATION FOR SUCCESS

Thirty-five years of study, practise and experience integrated these 6 lessons into the essential tools needed to have an advantage over other drummers. I say that to instill the importance of these foundation parts and not to brag or to instill a competitive attitude within the drummer. I have worked with over 100 "stars" of television, radio, and theatre. I also spent countless hours researching, writing and developing The Time Space and Drums Series. The basic techniques covered in Part 1 would normally take months or even years to integrate, but you have the opportunity to bypass years of expensive drum lessons to learn these basic fundamentals now.

This first part of the series is designed to be studied over a 6-week period and could save the student needless expenses in the long, and short term. Although that said, these methods are designed to be practised, either alongside any current tuition course or method you are currently undertaking or separate from other methods. The choice is yours and will depend largely on the seriousness of your drumming ambitions.

So, I urge you to master these tools today, to help you guarantee you'll be where you want to be tomorrow as a drummer.

The Time Space and Drums Series brings the future to you, NOW.

Regards,

Stephen Hawkins.

Free Audio Demonstrations

You should visit the following URL to download audio demonstrations of every exercise in this book as soon as possible. You will then receive additional tips and guidance through the included essence emails.

www.timespaceanddrums.com/tsd-1pa.html

DRUM ROLL, PLEASE! Getting Started

Welcome to Time Space and Drums Series Part 1 and thank you for choosing the program. After playing the drums for over 35 years, I decided I would like to pass on something of what I have learned along the way. I hope this series makes it easier and shortens the road between where you are now and where you want to go.

I learned my skills, like many drummers, by spending countless hours studying books, tapes, videos and watching and listening to other drummers. I designed this series to cut through some of the work, by helping you to pick up everything you need to know now and in years to come, as rapidly and effortlessly as possible. However, that doesn't mean that this is an easy road. In fact, by knowing the most useful exercises to learn at the beginning of your career, and mastering those exercises, I hope you will have more work to do as you become more in demands for your skills and abilities.

This series is designed to provide novice drummers with a SOLID FOUNDATION of drum know-how and then leads into more advanced stages of musicianship as the series progresses. The emphasis throughout will be on simplicity and versatility. Instead of slogging through a series of 1 hour, once a week lessons with an outside tutor for 2-3 years, at a cost of £1000-£2500, with few skills under your belt at the end, this program if you follow it as designed, will get you up and playing — and feeling perfectly at home behind the drum set — within a much shorter time.

Because of computers, tape machines etc., drummers can become threatened. Why? Simply because the average drummer cannot play to the standards required to become a working professional in today's world. It is therefore vital that the student understands implicitly the concepts of reading music, no matter the playing style he or she prefers. The drummer's skills can then be increased later more easily, by reading the more technical exercises.

Musical demonstrations are included within this program, but I urge you to totally understand this and all other series parts as just a book. Understand what's written from the explanations etc., from a theoretical point of view.

If your aim is to become a full-fledged professional drummer, employed in interesting, rewarding gigs, these lessons will provide you with the necessary skills and knowledge.

Too many drummers waste their first 2-3 years trying to learn all sorts of fancy, intricate rhythms, instead of practicing the genuinely useful although, perhaps fewer exciting drum skills. Sooner or later, they are criticized for not having the solid foundation of "Hands-On" experience, which is vital for success in the world of professional music.

It cannot be stressed enough that a drummer must have a solid background of practise, in the proper techniques. Just as a pilot's readiness is measured in the number of flying hours he has put in, a drummer, if he wants to achieve some modicum of success, must also be prepared to log in a lot of practise time. It's the only way to gain the "building blocks" on which to develop a larger vocabulary later on.

Start building your "house" of dreams on a solid foundation from the start.

As with everything else in life, you start with first things first. And the first rule in any game is to know the rules. You can then bend them into your own personal style later.

Some people, due to one of those annoying, uncanny twists of fate, just seem to have a natural gift for playing the drums. Don't be concerned about that. Whether or not you are one of those lucky few, stick with the exercises in the series, and when you've completed them all, I am confident that you will indeed find yourself to be one of those people. It will feel natural for you to sit at the drum set and play them —even if what you play is very basic. Advanced techniques are simply basic fundamentals played exceptionally well. And understood just as well.

Learn all the exercises, strive for some degree of perfection and you should have no problem achieving your goal of becoming a great drummer — with all the rewards and satisfaction that the career offers.

All your favorite drummers and mine are extremely versatile drummers and musicians. You may have only heard them specializing in one technique such as heavy rock, heavy metal, and so on, depending on what sort of music you listen to most. Behind the scenes, however, they are usually skilled in jazz drumming techniques and it is this that opens the door to integration of all drumming skills and creativity. It will also open doors to a wider world of employment opportunities.

It is, therefore, vital that you learn both types of drumming: rock and jazz. Neither has nor should have precedence over the other. They are equally important to know and master, no matter what music style you personally prefer. As stated, jazz techniques will make your rock drumming skills soar to new heights on an exponential level.

Good Luck! And Cheers to The Drummers of Tomorrow.

DRUM BUYERS GUIDE:

Equipment Guide: Drum Kits

Different standards and prices of drum kits are available for a wide range of specialized styles, including ROCK, JAZZ and FUSION. The more specialized, the higher the price. However, don't be misled by the variety available. Most drum stores stock a selection of kits for the beginner. After playing pearl drums for 25 years with a 3-year period playing others, I have found pearl drums to be the best for me. Pearl drums are tuneable to almost any playing style after a bit of experience and are great value for money. The Pearl Export Drum Kit is about the most practical, value for money kit on the market today. However, that is just my own personal taste.

The cost of a good drum kit would be around £600. I recently purchased a Pearl Export 5-piece kit which included stands, stool, pedals and a full set of Sabian Cymbals for £850. If you persist, you can usually walk away with a good deal. I saved around £300 on my Pearl export kit just by persisting and bargaining. Below is a diagram of the basic drum set up you should aim for.

You could purchase a second-hand kit for around £150, but if you can afford it, try to get yourself a new one as the expense in making the purchase will help strengthen your determination to learn how to play.

Electronic Drums

Several electronic drum kits are available, but personally, I don't get on with them. They are good for playing straight-ahead rhythms, but at the time of writing, when it comes to dynamics, they can't do the job, in my opinion. That's only my personal preference, but should you prefer the electronic kit then, by all means, get some good advice and try a few out before buying. A little research can save you a lot of time and money. In actual fact, the demonstrations included with this series were recorded on a Roland TD-6 Electronic kit. I did have a few problems getting the dynamics good enough, especially on the Accents Series part, but I did eventually manage to produce the demonstrations somewhat satisfactorily.

Sound Test:

When you try-out a drum set below £600, new or second-hand, have a fiddle around with the drum heads to find out whether it sounds good with the drum heads supplied. Usually, changing the drum heads can make a massive difference to the sound. I asked the shop to change the drum heads on my Pearl export Kit at very little cost, but the result was fantastic. I got the depth I wanted by simply changing the drum heads. Pin Stripe drumheads give a much deeper tone with less high ring pitch. Put a little gaffer tape on the heads to deaden the ring and they sound great; so great that anyone would think I was playing a £2000 drum kit.

Again, at the time of writing, you can get a good set of drum heads for around £35, depending on your personal choice. Take a drum to the shop and try a few drum heads out. But remember that with all the other equipment around, there will be a lot of ring from the drum no matter what head you try. So, use your imagination a little and imagine the sound with less ring. It's a good idea to get someone else to play the drum while you walk away and hear the drum from a distance. That way you're more likely to hear what the drum really sounds like.

Tips for Buying Second-hand Drums: If you find that a new drum kit runs over your available budget, check out your local newspapers for a good second-hand one. You should be able to get a good second-hand drum set for around £300 or less. Just give it a polish and it will look like new. Change the drum heads and it will sound good too.

After putting in the hours and practicing the Time, Space and Drums Series of books, I would suggest that you purchase the very best drum set you can afford. A Pearl Masters or Yamaha 9000R for instance. This will cost you around £2000, but the satisfaction from the sound and the reputation you get by playing a great kit along with your ability to give other musicians what they want to hear, the rewards should be well worth it. After all, by the time you've finished the whole series, you will have earned it. Your investment in yourself will give you the motivation to climb the ladder to greater success. But for now, let's get down to the nitty-gritty.

STRIKE UP THE BEAT: Beginning Pointers

Before you even pick up a stick, there are a few important things you should know. Here are some of the first basics to grasp and remember. These pointers should be observed throughout The Time Space and Drums Series and indeed throughout your career as a drummer.

1. GRAVITY: Seating Posture

If you sit like a slouch, you will play like one. Sit up straight, in a comfortable but business-like manner, back straight and thighs parallel to the floor. Of cause, both feet should be positioned correctly on the foot pedals (explained later). I highly recommend learning the Alexander Technique for the very best posture.

Both of your lower legs should be slightly angled giving you adequate distance from the drum set. Then, set your drum-stool to a comfortable height. Incorrect seating posture could cause you serious back problems later on, especially after long, grueling sessions at many nightly gigs. See Appendix 1 below for correct seating posture.

Appendix 1

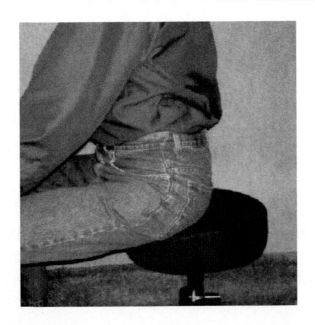

2. GRAVITY: Foot Positions

Most of the time I play with both heels positioned about 1-2 inches away from the foot pedal board. See Appendix 2 & 3. The whole leg moves up then down to strike the pedals, but the toes and balls of the feet NEVER leave the pedal board. After experimenting with this technique and employing it, you should be able to create the habit naturally and quite easily.

Appendix 2   Appendix 3

After establishing your foot position for both feet as previously explained, the next step is to learn how to hold the drumsticks. However, there is no rush. Time spent now correcting your foot positions will be well worth the effort.

The ultimate outcome of the positioning of the drums and seating posture is the balance. In that, I mean your backside becomes a fulcrum point or pivot point for you to sort of hover around the kit in a flowing fluid motion. But that will come later as you progress.

3: IRON GRIP CONTROL: Holding the Drumsticks

Holding the drumsticks is an art all of its own, which like many things in drumming, will take time to master. However, a good way to begin is to place one of your sticks across the palm of your right-hand, making sure that the butt or the thick end of the stick is overlapping your palm (wrist joints) by about 1 inch, as illustrated in appendix 4 below.

Appendix 4   Appendix 5

Then move your thumb across so that it is touching the stick (See appendix 5 above). Now wrap your other 4 fingers around the stick (See appendix 6).

When you have done this, turn your whole arm, hand and wrist so that your thumb is on top as shown in appendix 7 below.

Appendix 6   Appendix 7

Now, do exactly the same with your left-hand. So, every time you pick up the sticks to play the drums, you should have your sticks in your hand in the described position.

A little trick is to position both sticks in your hands and then before you hit the drum, squeeze the stick as tightly as possible. Then after about 1 minute, stop squeezing. You now have the correct grip of the sticks. It's not too tight that you might damage your wrist as you hit the drum, and it's not too loose so the stick might fall out of your hands. Try to maintain that grip every time you hit the drum, which is the next step.

Start by positioning your right-hand so that your stick is pointing upwards as described below. Then move the stick (turning your wrist slightly downwards) slowly towards the drum. Then stop halfway (See description below). Now, move your whole arm and wrist slowly towards the drum until the stick touches the drum. At this point, your arm should form a straight line with your wrist and hand.

Practise this movement slowly a few times with both hands and remember that you are creating habits (Good habits). So, don't rush.

When you are comfortable, you can strike the drum once, to begin with, examining each stroke for the right movement. Please note, that after hitting the drum for the first time, you should reverse the movements. That is, start with the stick touching the drum, then move it halfway up (note that the stick will help by bouncing off of the drum head). Then finally to the upright position.

After practicing the above method slowly, to begin with, you will become aware of the exact time that the stick hits the drum. At that point, you should bring the stick away from the drum straight away (again, it will bounce off the drum head).

If you just drop the stick on the drum, it will bounce off. It is that bounce that you are going to learn to control. The entire movement of the stick repeated over and over again would look something like this.

Stick up, stick halfway down, stick on the drum, bounce off again, Stick halfway up.

Stick up, stick halfway down, stick on the drum, bounce off again, Stick halfway up.

Stick up, stick halfway down, stick on the drum, bounce off again, Stick halfway up.

Stick up, stick halfway down, stick on the drum, bounce off again, Stick halfway up.

Stick up, stick halfway down, stick on the drum, bounce off again, Stick halfway up.

And so on.

Now, before you start studying and practicing lesson 1, you should practise the stick motion above for at least 1 week. To jump straight into lesson 1 would mean that you would start creating bad habits. You should learn good habits. Time spent now perfecting this method will save valuable time later on. So, spend 1 hour or more for a full week practicing hitting the drum with your right-hand, then the left-hand, then the right-hand then your left-hand and again with your right-hand. Alternate and repeat this until you become comfortable striking the drum.

Also, divide your time up and practise your foot technique as mentioned earlier. And remember that what goes for the hands goes for the feet also. By that I mean when the bass drum pedal hits the drum, you should immediately lift the weight off of your pedal to let the beater bounce off the bass drum head. Practise playing the right-foot and left-foot for a whole week also. Experiment with how it feels and how it sounds. Listen to the drums: they will tell your ears when they sound the best. You will then begin to develop a method that is comfortable and easy for you.

The techniques mentioned are the most basic fundamentals and should be practised over a long period.

Reread the last few paragraphs until you have everything I have mentioned in your mind. Understanding is what you are aiming for and by understanding, you are really visualizing the motions of feet and hands. You can then correct playing hands and feet issues or mistakes as you encounter them and as you begin to advance through the exercises in this book. Be content here to not be perfect at this point, knowing that later you will begin learning, practicing and perfecting rudiments to further improve everything you practise within the Time Space and Drums Series.

You should continue the "Holding Sticks and Foot Position" development for your whole drumming career. Practise and Master the BASICS as they will become VITAL as you progress. I will include a video of BASIC RUDIMENTS with this series, but I highly recommend you get yourself a copy of Dave Weckl's Back to Basics Video. It is probably the best Hand and Foot Technique Video around.

4: NO STICK TRICKS: First things first

The basic rock drumming techniques are covered in this book and should be integrated before moving on to book 2. The lessons are aimed at the beginner and intermediate level player, but can also be of use to the more advanced or accomplished drummer to use as a further improvement tool. Only when you have mastered the exercises at various volume levels and tempos should you begin to concentrate on developing a personal style. For now, simply be content with practicing the exercises in the order they are given, understanding and deciphering the written musical exercises, playing solidly and in time. Remember, perfection isn't the first step. **The science must come before the art?**

5: PUMP UP THE VOLUME: Listen to The Noise

Although it may cause problems with the neighbors, I recommend that at least, to begin with, you play everything loudly, that is, at the volume of the kit. You have much to accomplish and you won't need to worry about the volume that you're playing at. You can then learn how to control the volume by reducing the level over a period of time. You should aim to play everything quietly, prettily even, which not only causes less conflict with the neighbors but also gives you more control. To play loud is easy; to play almost silently is very difficult. But again, concentrate on the scientific method (getting the motions right and in time) before the technique and art or creative level of playing. Put another way... concentrate on the WHAT, not the HOW. Unless of course, you are an intermediate or advanced player, then you would concentrate on the HOW of what you play in order to improve further.

It might pay you to check out your practice environment first and let people know that you are learning how to play the drums and that they can expect the volume to gradually decrease as time goes on. You could try befriending anyone who might have a tendency to complain and get them on your side before you start. Once they know what you are trying to accomplish, they may become more tolerant of the noise. Try to schedule your practise time so that it doesn't conflict with the sleep needs of the rest of the world around you. Alternatively, get yourself a practise kit. You can then practise when you like.

6: THE BEAT GOES ON: Practising the Drums

I recommend that you practise for at least 1 hour per day. More if possible. It should be a time that you have put aside for the intention of practise. You will need a metronome to keep you in time, to begin with. You can then practise the exercises without a metronome to see how you're playing sounds and to try to keep in time. But in all cases throughout the Time Space and Drums Series, you will need a metronome; so, if you don't have one, practise the hands and feet exercises explained earlier until you get one. There are also apps you can download or online metronomes you can make use of.

Start with the metronome at 60 BPM (Beats Per Minute). Listen to the metronome for a few minutes until you understand its function, where the clicks are and how long the spaces are. You could try counting each click — 1, 2, 3, 4, 1, 2, 3, 4 — aloud, repeatedly.

Once you can count in time with the metronome, you can try exercise 1. It is played on the hi-hat cymbals with your right-hand. Remember to keep your left-foot pressed tightly enough on the hi-hat pedal so that the cymbals don't rattle together. The diamond symbol above each hi-hat beat represents each click of the metronome. Each time you strike the hi-hat cymbals with your right-hand, you should hear the metronome click. So, make sure that the metronome is loud enough. An electronic metronome which you can plug into a speaker or hi-fi system is recommended.

When you feel comfortable with exercise 1, try exercise 2. Exercise 2 includes adding the bass drum on beats 1 and 3, (1 and 3 refer to **1**, 2, **3**, 4 when you're counting along to the metronome). Then exercise 3.

Please DON'T move on to exercise 2 until you have a full understanding of exercise 1. Understanding of each exercise is paramount, in order to keep building the foundation you need. Remember the exercises get more difficult, so you must perfect each exercise in order to go on.

Once you have perfected lesson 1 at 60 BPM, try it at 70, then again at 80, then 90 and so on. When you get stiff, or you can't keep up, stop and have a break. Then start again from 60.

Do this with lesson 1 at different volumes as well as different tempos before moving on to lesson 2. I recommend at least 6 weeks to practise lessons 1-6 in this Part 1 book. They should be mastered before going on to the Part 2 book. This again should be practised for at least 6 weeks. You should then take 6 weeks of perfection practise before moving on to the Part 3 book. Then practise Parts 3 & 4 for 6 weeks each, then take a 6-week break to perfect them and so on. If you follow this advice and stick to practising, you won't be just a drummer in 2 years' time, you will be a very good drummer.

You will then have the tools to become a great drummer during the following few years.

Remember that you are aiming at building a solid foundation of drumming skills. Therefor, if you stick with the exercises until you can play them correctly and in time, your efforts will flow smoothly with the metronome. If you find, to begin with, that the metronome seems too slow or it rushes by, try slowing the metronome down or speeding it up slightly. You will, with trial and error, establish a comfortable learning speed, but you must remember that you are aiming to practise the exercises slow. This takes discipline. Discipline gives you time to reflect and to think about what you're doing the thought that gives you control.

After 15 or so years of playing with stars from television etc., I was never called a good drummer until I began striving to make things slower, giving me time to analyze what I was doing in order to see all of the imperfections in my playing. I could then eliminate those imperfections. "Be patient." Speed and style will come with time. The more you slow it down and rip it apart now to perfect each exercise, the more abundant will be your speed and style later.

7: WHAT'S THAT NOISE? Music Notation

Before you begin exercise 1, lesson 1 below is a map of the musical notes, and where they are written on a musical "staff" or "stave."

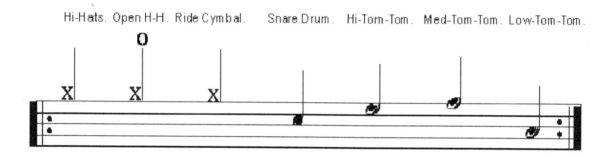

Notice that the ride cymbal and hi-hat cymbals use the same sign. To avoid confusion throughout the Time Space and Drums Series, I will use HH (Hi-Hats) or Cym (Ride Cymbal) to distinguish between the two.

Notice that the above diagram starts and ends with a thick vertical line, followed by a thinner vertical line then two dots. This means that you repeat everything in-between those symbols. This applies to every exercise throughout this book. Repeat the exercises until you are comfortable playing them. In the demonstration audio, I repeat each bar twice but you should play each exercise repetitively until you can play them all smoothly. Other abbreviations used throughout the books include:

RH, Right-hand
LH, Left-hand
RF, Right Foot
LF, Left Foot
SD, Snare Drum
BD, Bass Drum
HT, Hi Tom-Tom
MT, Medium Tom-Tom

LT, Low Tom-Tom

8: I GOT RHYTHM: Measuring the Beat

Most of the time as a professional drummer, you will be asked to play in 4/4 time, accordingly. That is how most of the rhythms in this series part have been written. This means that there are 4, crotchets or 1/4 notes per bar. The top figure 4 (First number 4) tells you how many of the notes are in a bar, and the bottom figure (Second number 4) tells you what kind of note they are.

Another example would be 7/8 for instance. This tells you that there are 7 notes in a bar and that they are quavers or 1/8th notes. In 5/4, there are 5 notes in a bar, and they would all be crotchets or 1/4 notes, but don't get into a tangle about this just yet...

Below is a diagram showing the notes, their values and their equivalent rests. After you study the following diagram, it should be obvious that after drawing a vertical line down from 1, 2, 3 and 4, that there are 4 crotchets (or 1/4 notes) in the time signature of 4/4. Eight (8) Quavers (or 1/8th notes) and 16 semi-quavers (or 1/16th notes) in 1 bar of 4/4 music as the diagram below demonstrates 4/4 music timing. Looking at it another way, there are 2 1/8th notes to each 1/4 note, and 4 1/16th notes to each 1/4 note.

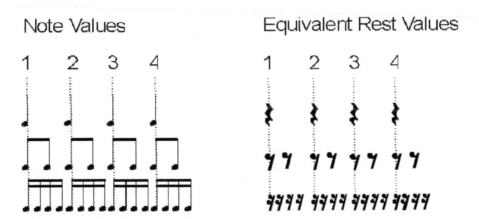

Please don't go any further until you fully understand what I have just written, and what I am trying to say. Let it become clear in your mind before moving on. Also, try to recognize the note and rest symbols as you see them (memorize them, and remember these are the building blocks).

At this point, go to page 47 and read the Understanding Rudiments section. You can then return here and then move onto the next page and then begin lesson one.

9: ATTI-DUDE: Walking the Walk

How you feel about yourself, your life, your dreams, your goals, your skills and talents as a drummer are very important. It is probably the single most important fact; apart from the exercises themselves, of course. If you're serious about becoming a professional drummer with a working band, start right now, by acting as if you have already made it.

Eliminate the negatives, be positive. Be "Up-Beat." Set yourself a goal for the day and approach it, not as if it were a tedious chore to get over with, but an enjoyable experience that you look forward to. Set a goal and achieve it. This will spur you on to the next, and the next, and so on.

You could, for example, set the goal of completing lesson 1, Part 1 in a week. Divide the lesson into 7 parts (7 days), then set out to reach each daily goal. Do this with all of the books in the series and you can, with confident control, know that by the time you complete the whole series that you will be an accomplished well-rounded drummer.

Either way, you'll get there. You have the building blocks, now start building a solid foundation. If you've taken the trouble to practise your hands and feet techniques, go to Lesson 1 now and start practising exercise 1.

Remember to visit the following URL to download audio demonstrations of every exercise in this book and to receive the Essence emails.

www.timespaceanddrums.com/tsd-1pa.html

Lesson 1

Quarter Note Rock Beat & Drum-fills

Exercise 1

Begin by setting your metronome to a slow tempo, (60 BPM). The symbol " " represents 1 click from the metronome. When you are ready, count 1, 2, 3, 4 continuously, until you can count evenly, and on time with the click. Then with your right-hand on the hi-hat cymbals proceed to play exercise 1. Simply strike the hi-hat cymbals on every beat of the click.

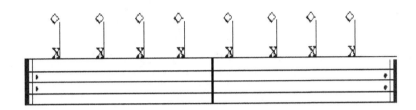

Exercise 2

Now add the bass drum on beats 1 and 3. Remember to count along with the right hi-hat beats you played in exercise 1. It may be easier to play exercise 1 repeatedly until you can mentally see and hear where the bass drum beats go.

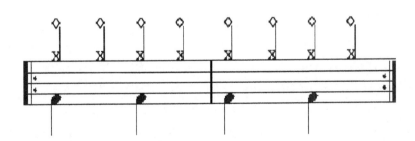

Exercise 3

Now add the snare drum on beats 2 and 4. Again, play exercise 2 repeatedly until you can mentally see and hear where the snare drum beats go.

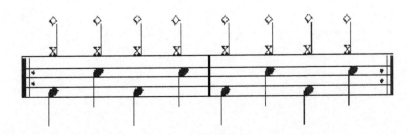

Congratulations, you've just played your first drum rhythm. Practice it at all volume levels and all tempos before going any further. Perfect it as far as possible.

Exercise 4

This time play the right-hand over on the ride cymbal. It is the exact same rhythm as exercise 1.

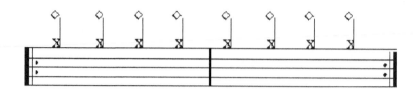

Exercise 5

Now play your left-foot on the hi-hat cymbals on beats 1, 2, 3, and 4, as indicated.

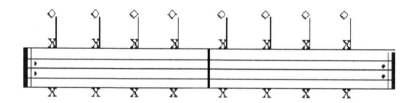

Exercise 6

Now add the bass drum on beats 1 and 3. Remember again to count along with the left-foot hi-hat beats you played in exercise 5. It may be easier to play exercise 5 repeatedly until you can mentally see and hear where the bass drum beats go.

To help you get this exercise, you might want to practice playing just the pattern that you play with your feet, to begin with.

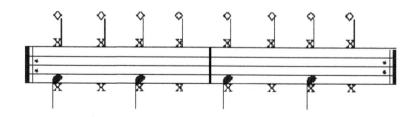

Exercise 7

Now add the snare drum on beats 2 and 4. Again, play exercise 6 repeatedly until you can mentally see and hear where the snare drum beats go in exercise 7 below.

Exercise 8

Now for the tricky part. If you go back to the notation examples (page 16) you will see that different notes have different values. 1/4 note, 1/8th note, and 1/16th note. There are 4 x 1/4 notes in a bar, 8 x 1/8th notes and 16 x 1/16th notes in a bar of 4/4 music. Up until now, you have just played 1/4 notes. Look at the exercises covered so far and you will see that there are 4 quarter notes in each bar. You would count 1, 2, 3, 4, and so on.

However, if the notes were 1/8th notes played throughout the bar you would count 1 and, 2 and, 3 and, 4 and. Or 1 +, 2 +, 3 +, 4 +. 1, 2, 3 or 4 on the beat, and "and" or "+" off the beat, or in-between the quarter notes. Refer to page 16 again to see what I just explained to you in words.

With 1/16th notes, however, we count 1 e and a, 2 e and a, 3 e and a, 4 e and a. Or, "1 e + a", "2 e + a", "3 e + a ", "4 e + a".

Count this over and over again and you will begin to hear the 1, 2, 3 and 4 clearly, with the "e + a" evenly spaced between 1, 2, 3 and 4. You will then hear clearly what exercise 8 sounds like. Again, refer to page 16 to see the explanation above as a musical notation diagram.

You play it using alternative sticking RLRL, RLRL, RLRL, RLRL.

So, let's have a go.

You should practice the movements of your arms played alternatively on a cushion or soft surface until you have the alternate flowing movements of your hands figured out.

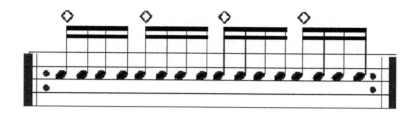

Exercise 9

This time, add the bass drum on beats 1, 2, 3 and 4. Again you may like to try playing the bass drum for a few bars until you get used to playing 1, 2, 3 and 4 on the bass drum.

Exercise 10

Now play the same drum-fill around the snare drum and tom-toms. 4 beats on each drum. 4 on the SD, 4 on the HT, 4 on the MT and 4 on the LT. Because you are playing RLRL, RLRL, RLRL, RLRL. You will notice that there are 2 right-hands on each drum. Try just playing the right-hand strokes, 2 on each drum. These are 1/8th notes. You will also notice that your hands and arms move in a circular motion. When you feel comfortable just playing the right-hand, try adding the left-hand in-between each right-hand stroke.

Exercise 11

Once you are used to playing exercises 1 through 10, try the following exercise. Play 3 bars exercise 3, then a drum-fill (exercise 10) around the tom-toms. Then 3 bars exercise 3 then a drum-fill. Keep this going until you can play it smoothly before going on to exercise 12, a3 and beyond.

Exercise 12

Now do the same thing again, but this time play exercise 7 for 3 bars, then a drum-fill (exercise 10). You should try to play the hi-hat throughout the drum-fill too. Along with the bass drum. But this may take some practice at first.

Exercise 13

Now try playing the drum-fill on beats 2, 3 and 4 of the fourth bar. This will all take practice, and working out, but the reward will be worth it. Count your way through it. It is a good idea to be able to hear the exercise in your head before you eventually get it right. Understanding what is written is the key. This will take some study.

Exercise 14

Now try playing exercise 7 for 3 bars then the fill on beats 2, 3, and 4 of bar four.

Exercise 15

Now play exercise 3 for 3 bars, then play the drum-fill on beats 3 and 4 of bar 4.

Exercise 16

Now play exercise 7 for 3 bars, then play the drum-fill on beats 3 and 4 of bar 4.

Exercise 17

This time play exercise 3 for 3 bars, then play the drum-fill on beat 4 of bar 4. The fill is played on the SD only.

Exercise 18

Now play exercise 7 for 3 bars, then play the drum-fill on beat 4 of bar 4.

Lesson 2

1/8th Note Rock Beat & Drum-fills

Exercise 1

Again, begin by setting your metronome to a slow tempo, (60 BPM). When you are ready, count 1, 2, 3, 4 continuously, until you can count evenly, and on time with the click. Then with your right-hand on the hi-hat cymbals proceed to play exercise 1.

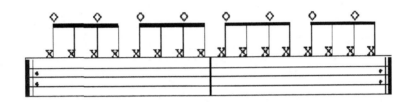

Exercise 2

Now add the bass drum on beats 1 and 3. Remember to count along with the right hi-hat beats you played in exercise 1. It may be easier to play exercise 1 repeatedly until you can mentally see and hear where the bass drum beats go.

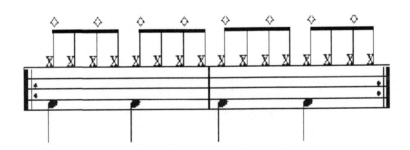

Exercise 3

Now add the snare drum on beats 2 and 4. Again, play exercise 2 repeatedly until you can mentally see and hear where the snare drum beats go.

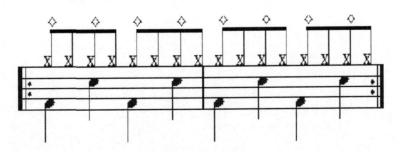

Congratulations, you've now played the second drum rhythm. Practice it at all volume levels and all tempos before going any further. Perfect it. Practice it at all volume levels and all tempos before going any further. Perfect it as much as you are able but be comfortable with it at least.

Exercise 4

This time play the right-hand over on the ride cymbal. It is the exact same rhythm as exercise 1.

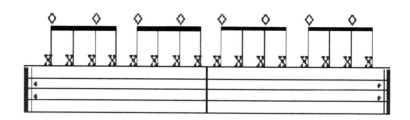

Exercise 5

Now play your left-foot on the hi-hat cymbals on beats 1, 2, 3, and 4, as indicated.

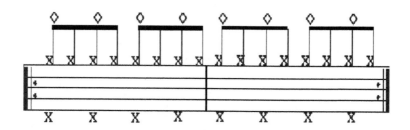

Exercise 6

Now add the bass drum on beats 1 and 3. Remember to count along with the right hi-hat beats you played in exercise 1. It may be easier to play exercise 5 repeatedly until you can mentally see and hear where the bass drum beats go.

To help you get this exercise, you might want to practice playing just your feet, to begin with.

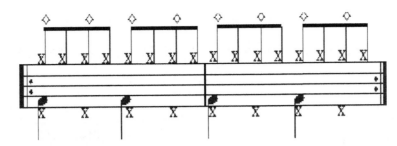

Exercise 7

Now add the snare drum on beats 2 and 4. Again, play exercise 6 repeatedly until you can mentally see and hear where the snare drum beats go.

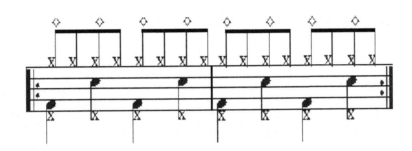

Exercise 8

Once you are used to playing exercises 1 through 7, try the following exercise. Play 3 bars exercise 3, then the drum-fill you learned in lesson 1. Keep this going until you can play it smoothly before going on.

Exercise 9
Now do the same thing again, but this time play exercise 7 for 3 bars, then the drum-fill.

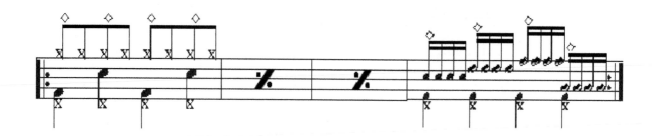

Exercise 10
Now try playing exercise 3 for 3 bars then the drum-fill on beats 2, 3 and 4 of the fourth bar.

Exercise 11
Now try playing exercise 7 for 3 bars then the fill on beats 2, 3, and 4 of bar four.

Exercise 12
Now play exercise 3 for 3 bars, then play the drum-fill on beats 3 and 4 of bar 4.

Exercise 13

Now play exercise 7 for 3 bars, then play the drum-fill on beats 3 and 4 of bar 4.

Exercise 14

This time play exercise 3 for 3 bars, then play the drum-fill on beat 4 of bar 4. Again, the fill is played on the SD only.

Exercise 15

Now play exercise 7 for 3 bars, then play the drum-fill on beat 4 of bar 4.

Lesson 3

1/16ᵗʰ Note Rock Beat & Drum-fills

Exercise 1

Again, begin by setting your metronome to a slow tempo, (60 BPM). When you are ready, count 1, 2, 3, 4 continuously, until you can count evenly, and on time with the click. Then with your right-hand on the hi-hat cymbals proceed to play exercise 1.

In lesson 1 we played a 1/4 note rock beat, in lesson 2 we doubled the hi-hat up to play a 1/8ᵗʰ note beat.

Now we're going to double up again and play a 1/16ᵗʰ note beat. The right-hand on the HH is the exact same rhythm as the drum-fill we've been playing. You may have to slow the metronome down a little to learn these exercises.

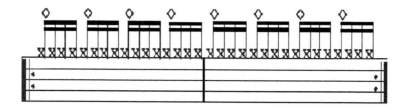

Exercise 2

Now add the bass drum on beats 1 and 3. Remember to count along with the right hi-hat beats you played in exercise 1. The count if you remember is "1 e and a, 2 e and a, 3 e and a, 4 e and a, etc. It may be easier to play exercise 1 repeatedly until you can mentally see and hear where the bass drum beats go.

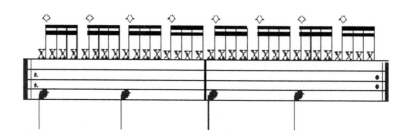

Exercise 3

Now add the snare drum on beats 2 and 4. Again, play exercise 2 repeatedly until you can mentally see and hear where the snare drum beats go.

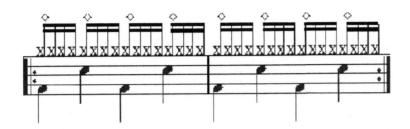

Congratulations, you've now played the second drum rhythm. Practice it at all volume levels and all tempos before going any further. Perfect it as far as you can before moving on.

Exercise 4

This time play the right-hand over on the ride cymbal. It is the exact same rhythm as exercise 1.

Exercise 5

Now play your left-foot on the hi-hat cymbals on beats 1, 2, 3, and 4, as indicated.

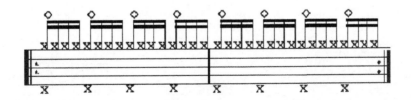

Exercise 6

Now add the bass drum on beats 1 and 3. Remember to count along with the left-foot hi-hat beats you played in exercise 5. It may be easier to play exercise 5 repeatedly until you can mentally see and hear where the bass drum beats go. You may even need to play only the vertical notes throughout the bar. For example, right-hand, right foot and left foot together. Followed by right-hand on its own and so on just until you develop the coordination required to play the beat.

Then, to help you get this exercise more smoothly, you might want to practice playing just your feet, to begin with.

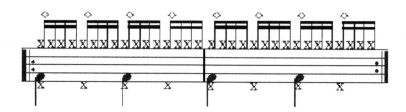

Exercise 7

Now add the snare drum on beats 2 and 4. Again, play exercise 6 repeatedly until you can mentally see and hear where the snare drum beats go.

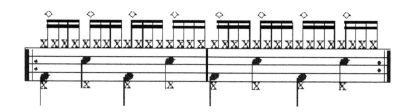

Exercise 8

Once you are used to playing exercises 1 through 7, try the following exercise. Play 3 bars exercise 3, then the drum-fill you learned in lesson 1. Keep this going until you can play it smoothly before going on.

Exercise 9

Now do the same thing again, but this time play exercise 7 for 3 bars, then the drum-fill.

Exercise 10

Now try playing exercise 3 for 3 bars then the drum-fill on beats 2, 3 and 4 of the fourth bar.

Exercise 11

Now try playing exercise 7 for 3 bars then the fill on beats 2, 3, and 4 of bar four.

Exercise 12

Now play exercise 3 for 3 bars, then play the drum-fill on beats 3 and 4 of bar 4.

Exercise 13

Now play exercise 7 for 3 bars, then play the drum-fill on beats 3 and 4 of bar 4.

Exercise 14

This time play exercise 3 for 3 bars, then play the drum-fill on beat 4 of bar 4. Again, the fill is played on the SD only.

Exercise 15

Now play exercise 7 for 3 bars, then play the drum-fill on beat 4 of bar 4.

Lesson 4

1/16th Note Variation 1 & Drum-fills

Exercise 1

The following exercises are slightly more difficult. They are similar to those covered in lesson 3. However, this time the last 1/16th note in every group of 4 is missing. Instead of counting "1", "e", "and", "a". The count is "1", "e", "and" (then a silent "a"). For instance, if you count aloud continuously 1, 2, 3, 4 but leave the 4 silent, then speed your count up to as fast as you can. By listening to your voice, you will know how these exercises sound. Try it before attempting then mastering these next exercises.

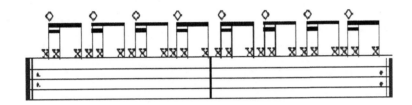

Exercise 2

Now add the bass drum on beats 1 and 3. Remember to count along with the right hi-hat beats you played in exercise 1. It may be easier to play exercise 1 repeatedly until you can mentally see and hear where the bass drum beats go.

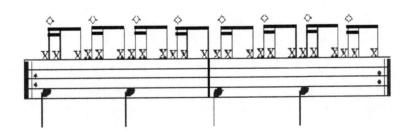

Exercise 3

Now add the snare drum on beats 2 and 4. Again, play exercise 2 repeatedly until you can mentally see and hear where the snare drum beats go.

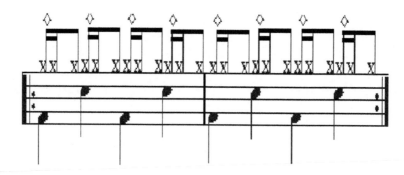

Practice exercise 3 at all volume levels and all tempos before going any further. Perfect it as far as possible.

Exercise 4

This time play the right-hand over on the ride cymbal. It is the exact same rhythm as exercise 1.

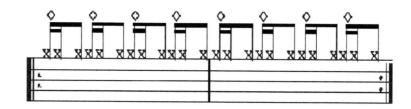

Exercise 5

Now play your left-foot on the hi-hat cymbals on beats 1, 2, 3, and 4, as indicated.

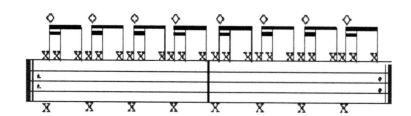

Exercise 6

Now add the bass drum on beats 1 and 3. Remember to count along with the right hi-hat beats you played in exercise 1.

It may be easier to play exercise 5 repeatedly until you can mentally see and hear where the bass drum beats go.

Again, to help you get this exercise, you might want to practice playing just your feet, to begin with.

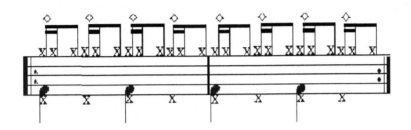

Exercise 7

Now add the snare drum on beats 2 and 4. Again, play exercise 6 repeatedly until you can mentally see and hear where the snare drum beats go in exercise 7 below.

Exercise 8

Once you are used to playing exercises 1 through 7, try the following exercise. Play 3 bars exercise 3, then the drum-fill you learned in lesson 1. Keep this going until you can play it smoothly before going on.

Exercise 9

Now do the same thing again, but this time play exercise 7 for 3 bars, then the drum-fill.

Exercise 10

Now play exercise 3 for 3 bars then try playing the drum-fill on beats 2, 3 and 4 of the fourth bar.

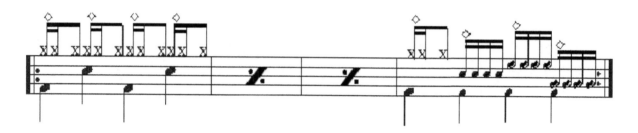

Exercise 11

Now try playing exercise 7 for 3 bars then the fill on beats 2, 3, and 4 of bar four.

Exercise 12

Now play exercise 3 for 3 bars, then play the drum-fill on beats 3 and 4 of bar 4.

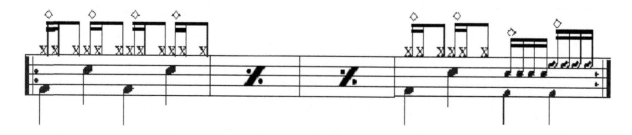

Exercise 13

Now play exercise 7 for 3 bars, then play the drum-fill on beats 3 and 4 of bar 4.

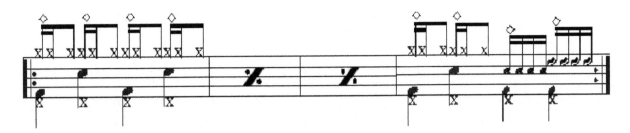

Exercise 14

This time play exercise 3 for 3 bars, then play the drum-fill on beat 4 of bar 4. Again, the fill is played on the SD only.

Exercise 15

Now play exercise 7 for 3 bars, then play the drum-fill on beat 4 of bar 4.

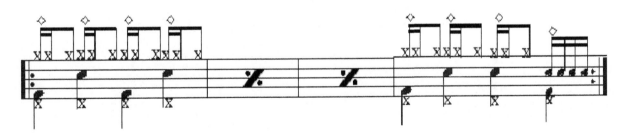

Lesson 5

1/16ᵗʰ Note Variation 2 & Drum-fills

Exercise 1

This one is slightly trickier still. This time every second 1/16ᵗʰ note is missing from each group of 4. So instead of "1", "e", "and", "a".   The "e" is silent. So, we get "1", "rest", "and", "a". If you hit the snare drum on "1", "and", "a". And whilst singing the count you leave the "e" silent; you will know what this exercise sounds like. So, take it away.

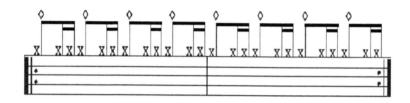

Exercise 2

Now add the bass drum on beats 1 and 3. Remember to count along with the right hi-hat beats you played in exercise 1. It may be easier to play exercise 1 repeatedly until you can mentally see and hear where the bass drum beats go.

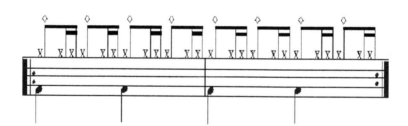

Exercise 3

Now add the snare drum on beats 2 and 4. Again, play exercise 2 repeatedly until you can mentally see and hear where the snare drum beats go.

Now practice it at all volume levels and all tempos before going any further.

Exercise 4

This time play the right-hand over on the ride cymbal. It is the exact same rhythm as exercise 1.

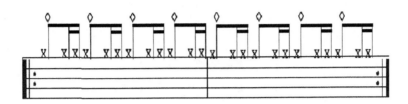

Exercise 5

Now play your left-foot on the hi-hat cymbals on beats 1, 2, 3, and 4, as indicated.

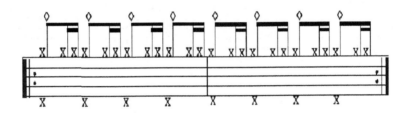

Exercise 6

Now add the bass drum on beats 1 and 3. Remember to count along with the left-foot hi-hat beats you played in exercise 5. It may be easier to play exercise 5 repeatedly until you can mentally see and hear where the bass drum beats go.

As usual, to help you get this exercise, you might want to practice playing just your feet, to begin with.

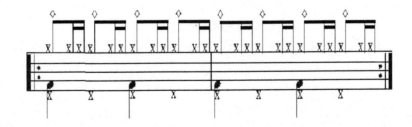

Exercise 7

Now add the snare drum on beats 2 and 4. Again, play exercise 6 repeatedly until you can mentally see and hear where the snare drum beats go.

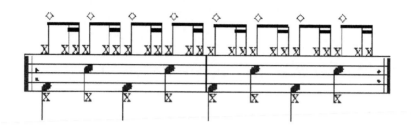

Exercise 8

Once you are used to playing exercises 1 through 7, try the following exercise. Play 3 bars exercise 3, then the drum-fill you learned in lesson 1. Keep this going until you can play it smoothly before going on.

Exercise 9

Now do the same thing again, but this time play exercise 7 for 3 bars, then the drum-fill.

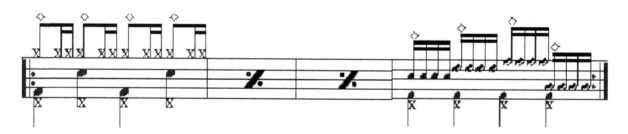

Exercise 10

Now play exercise 3 for 3 bars then try playing the drum-fill on beats 2, 3 and 4 of the fourth bar.

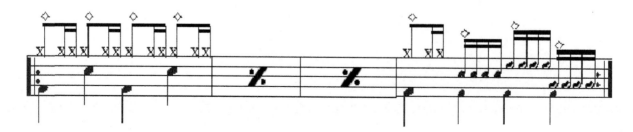

Exercise 11

Now try playing exercise 7 for 3 bars then the fill on beats 2, 3, and 4 of bar four.

Exercise 12

Now play exercise 3 for 3 bars, then play the drum-fill on beats 3 and 4 of bar 4.

Exercise 13

Now play exercise 7 for 3 bars, then play the drum-fill on beats 3 and 4 of bar 4.

Exercise 14

This time play exercise 3 for 3 bars, then play the drum-fill on beat 4 of bar 4. Again, the fill is played on the SD only.

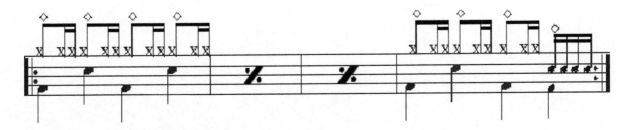

Exercise 15

Now play exercise 7 for 3 bars, then play the drum-fill on beat 4 of bar 4.

Lesson 6

1/8th Note Variation Rock Beat & Drum-fills

Exercise 1

Again, begin by setting your metronome to a slow tempo, (60 BPM). When you are ready, count 1, 2, 3, 4 continuously, until you can count evenly, and on time with the click. Then with your left-foot on the hi-hat pedal proceed to play exercise 1. This time play the hi-hat cymbals with your LF on beats 1, 2, 3 and 4, (every beat of the click).

The count as mentioned previously in lesson 1 is, 1 and, 2 and, 3 and, 4 and. But you only play the RH hi-hat on the "and" of every beat (1, 2, 3, 4). Play evenly and remember: The "and" falls exactly between 1, 2, 3 and 4. You can start by just playing the H.H. with your left-foot. Then every time the h-hats are open hit the hi-hats with your right-hand.

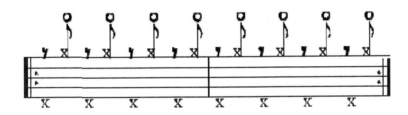

Exercise 2

Now add the bass drum on beats 1 and 3. Remember to count along with the left-foot hi-hat beats you played in exercise 1. It may be easier to play exercise 1 repeatedly until you can mentally see and hear where the bass drum beats go.

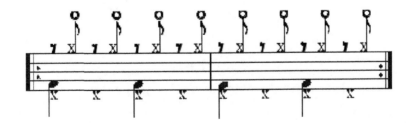

Exercise 3

Now add the snare drum on beats 2 and 4. Again, play exercise 2 repeatedly until you can mentally see and hear here the snare drum beats go.

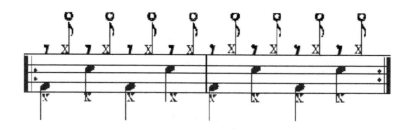

Exercise 4

Once you are used to playing exercises 1 to 3, try the following exercise.
Play 3 bars exercise 3, then the drum-fill you learned in lesson 1. Keep this going until you can play it smoothly before going on.

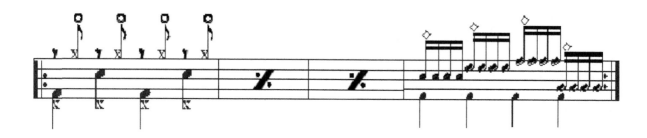

Exercise 5

Now do the same thing again, but this time play the drum-fill on beats 2, 3 and 4.

Exercise 6

Now try playing the drum-fill on beats 3 and 4 of the fourth bar.

Exercise 7

Now try playing the fill on beat 4 of bar four.

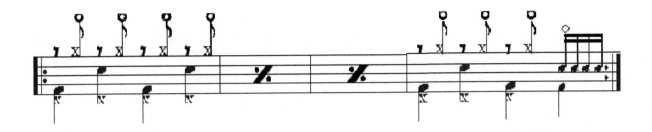

UNDERSTANDING RUDIMENTS

Single Stroke Roll

Okay, so I have a confession to make. I am terrible at playing some rudiments; although I say that I am pretty good at playing others, I must confess here that I could have taken them a lot further, which is always the case with rudiments.

But before we get into the rudiments themselves, let me address an issue many people have come to accept as normal when it comes to learning and mastering anything, including the drums. However, to illustrate this, I will tell you a brief story.

Ten minutes before I began writing this section, I put myself in the shoes of a complete beginner who was just starting out then did a quick search on the web and discovered a drum fill tutorial video. This demonstrated and confirmed what I have said several times previously about spending too much time watching videos in order to learn, unless you are pretty good from the start...

I digress: the tutorial I found was highly polished and was indeed a great video. However, the video was for the complete beginner who didn't have any experience or skill with playing drum-fills. I immediately believed that the drummer was going to cover the drum fills within this book. I actually felt a little down because I thought my time had been wasted writing this and subsequent books in the series as the ideas I was promoting were already covered in free videos online.

After feeling slightly depressed, I continued to watch the video and the presenter went on to say, "This is the most basic drum fill as we are starting from the complete beginner's point of view." I thought right then that he is definitely going to teach the same system that I am here.

After spending 3 minutes explaining what he was going to teach, which could have been said in about 15 seconds or less, he proceeded to play the drum fill. I was surprised as he didn't play the most basic drum fill at all. It was basic yes but not the most basic. He had started from step 4 or 5 in the drum fill process. My depressed feelings were lifted and so I skipped through the video and realized that he didn't give just one drum fill, he gave several.

Woah, I thought, *you said this was for the complete beginner but then went on to throw several drum-fills*. I believe this was a marketing choice to give more value. But, giving that value to the complete beginner was a bad decision in my opinion. Why?

Well, for the same reason that those kinds of videos cause problems for most people learning most things. Throwing several drum fills that you are informed are for the complete beginner yet start at step 4 or 5 then progress to include several more drum fills will have one of two possible effects.

First, it will bog you down for a couple of weeks with hardly any feelings of accomplishment, which demonstrates that the video caused confusion and was not uplifting for you the student. This is simply because of the second effect: Being overwhelmed. The feeling of being overwhelmed will destroy your progress if you decide to struggle onward through the mire of confusion that was placed before you as a complete beginner.

I have done something similar in this book but I have done it very differently. I covered 6 drum beats that are variations of each other beat but presented them as separate lessons. So, the student takes one lesson chunk at a time and progresses through the teachings and exercises of that lesson, one step at a time, until the lesson is completed. At which point the student should stick with the contents of that lesson for at least 1 week, practising a minimum of one hour per day. Remember: repetition is the road to mastery.

This may seem quite boring but as you progress and improve the contents of each lesson, you will feel more accomplished and hopeful of the coming lessons and the results you gain from those lessons.

The assumption made by the presenter of the video I just mentioned was that you are here to practise. The assumption that I make is that you are here for results, and yes, it will take practise to achieve those results. However, once you master the drum fills within these 6 lessons, you will be able to turn to the video and play all of those drum-fills in a few minutes without feeling confused or overwhelmed. It has everything to do with what you learn and practise and nothing to do with how much you learn or try to learn in a haphazard or confused way.

It is important that you get the issue of overwhelmingness out of the way right at the start of this book and anything else that you do in life. You see, being overwhelmed is not a cause in itself. It is the effect of a cause. Remove that cause and you remove the effect of being overwhelmed all together.

So, what is the cause of overwhelmingness? It's quite simple: being overwhelmed is the effect of concentrating on all of the steps that need to be done, instead of the *one step* that needs doing. It is practising step 1, yet being focused on all twenty steps, for example.

To illustrate, look at what we said about the drum fill tutorial video, the presenter gave you several drum fills in one lesson. The Time Space and Drums lessons give you one subject, exercise or exercises to practise within the same concept. You are therefore concentrating your focus on one thing at a time and not several which removes feelings of being overwhelmed all together.

If I gave the complete beginner 12 books that taught him how to build a solid rock drumming foundation, the student would most likely do nothing with the books as the feelings of being overwhelmed would stop him from making any progress at all.

The Single Stroke

So, now we have that out of the way, let's get down to the first rudiment. It should be noted that this whole book is centered around this one rudiment. It is the most basic rudiment and therefore used through just about everything that you do on the drums and as the most basic fundamental it needs to be practised over many years in order to improve and perfect.

This rudiment is really just hitting the drum once. That's it.

We call this a stroke, or a single stroke. This single stroke or hand movement should be practised individually with each of the two hands before doing anything else on the drums.

Turn now to the Holding the Drumsticks section beginning on page 9 and follow the instructions for holding the drumsticks. When you have the basic movements internalized, you can practise the movements a few times.

After practising the basic arm and hand movements as described, it is time to turn the single stroke into a single stroke roll.

The Single Stroke Roll

The single stroke roll is as it sounds. Do a single stroke with the right-hand and then do a single stroke with the left-hand all on the same drum or practice pad.

You then simply repeat those 2 strokes so the pattern begins to look like this:

R L, R L, R L, R L.

If you look at the notation diagram on page 16, you can see that the above exercise includes 8 strokes or notes and if you look at the notation diagram on page 16, you can see that the single stroke exercise above is a 1/8th note exercise. i.e., 8 x 1/8th notes in a single bar.

If we play the exercise again using twice as many notes (16), you see that the exercise becomes a 1/16th note exercise.

R L R L, R L R L, R L R L, R L R L.

Both of the examples above are played at the same speed but one has 8 notes in a bar and the other has 16 notes in a bar or the notes/strokes are doubled.

You can double up again and have 32 x 1/32nd notes in the bar but that is beyond the scope of this initial set of lessons and it is enough to understand the contents of the Measuring the Beat section on page 16.

Reread this whole Single Stroke Roll section to make absolutely sure that you understand the notation chart and values. Although each exercise is played at the same tempo, there are 8 x 1/8th notes in a bar and 16 x 1/16th notes in a bar. Now, return to the beginning of the book and move on to the first set of exercises in lesson 1.

Featured Drummer Recommendations

Dave Weckl

For the most part, I have used the name Dave Weckl throughout the complete Time Space and Drums Series as a reference point, in particular, pointing to a specific video of his, Back to Basics. In the beginning and for the drummer who has been playing for less than 2 years, I strongly suggest sticking to this one video of Dave's rather than using others he has produced.

Don't get me wrong, they all have value but until the techniques within the Back to Basics video are solidified within the drummer, I would strongly advise sticking to that particular video in the beginning, at least as a primary source and main source of study and practise.

You can then add The Next Step techniques after a few months of concentrating on the Back to Basics video content.

And again, after a few months, add the Contemporary Drummer Plus One package followed by the Evolution Series. But bear in mind that with the exception of the Contemporary Drummer package, each of these videos in one form or another will take the drummer back to the beginning, or back to basics so to speak.

If you remember, I view drumming and everything else as a journey from the beginning to the end and then back to the beginning again in a never-ending cycle.

Of course, this is so the student drummer can build his skills over time and is obviously subjective. It is up to the individual of course but please note that the recommendations I make are purely to give the student drummer time to practise the techniques within the previously mentioned videos.

I wasn't exposed to those videos in my early years and so can only make suggestions based on my own experience and you should act on your own experience too.

In that, I see the Back to Basics video as a more advanced technique after the student drummer has learned how to actually play the drums in the first place to at least intermediate level. He can then greatly improve his playing and better execute what he had previously learned before practicing the Back to Basics techniques. The title does suggest that the drummer already knows something about drumming and hence returns Back to the Basics where he once began.

If I was still at the beginning myself, I would most likely learn the techniques and pay attention to them but spend most of my time learning coordination after developing the foundation techniques. The Time Space and Drums Series includes coordination exercises as the beginning drummer develops. I say this because the techniques within Back to Basics are really basic yet really advanced based on your ability to play and master them. In other words, it will most likely take a few years and beyond to master those techniques and so the student should not get bogged down in taking them on too early. Although of course the opposite is also true and the student should get to know the techniques but as suggested not get bogged down by them and to instead study other areas, returning at specific benchmarks to those techniques.

But that isn't to say that the beginner or intermediate drummer should avoid these techniques altogether. They are very important and so at the very least it is worth laying some roots in the beginning and then "to be continued" as you grow and develop as a drummer, and that applies to all of the techniques covered in all of the videos I have mentioned.

Back to Basics & The Next Step

As a guide, it would be a good idea to use Dave's first two videos (Back to Basics and The Next Step) as the First Step. Then 6 months later, after you have dug some roots so to speak, begin to integrate The Evolution Series to your schedule which becomes the real next step.

Again, this is all subjective and different drummers will completely disagree and say you should get all of the books and all of the videos and go through them piece by piece on an alternating schedule. However, I strongly suggest that the beginner and intermediate drummer stick to one video, book or system at a time until those techniques have been mastered to some degree at least.

Some Things to Check out

Referring back to my own experience regarding Dave Weckl's drumming, in particular, my introduction to him as a master drummer I highly recommend The Chick Corea Electric Band album – Electric City. I recommend this very advanced album for a simple reason. That although acoustic, electronic kit (bugs) is a musical masterpiece, and by that, I am referring to the simple fact that although Dave plays some ridiculous rhythms and fills throughout, it clearly shows that the actual sound of the kit comes above all else. The drum sound fits the music if you will.

I have stated before in Modern Drumming Concepts that the mind of the drumming is a secondary focus as a beginner and intermediate player walks the road to becoming a better drummer and that is true. However, it serves to at least experience the mind of the drummer or more appropriately, the mind of the drumming.

I recommend the Electric City album for the simple reason that it is a masterpiece in mind and body drumming and by that, I mean that there is complete harmony between the technical mathematically intricate rhythms and the mind or sound that is produced.

This suggests that to some degree at least, complex drumming and drum-fills etc. are sacrificed for the good of the scientific root of the musical, and by that, I mean mathematical exactness and what fits the music and serves the music best.

Saying that the drumming is still very complex which shows the brilliance of that particular album. Of course, other albums demonstrate this but many don't do it so well.

The Featured Drummer section within each of the books in the series is not intended as a history and or biography of the drummer in question; instead, it is more of a reference as to how that drummer can help you look at your own drumming and hopefully how you can learn to play the drums a whole lot better. And remember that the Time Space and Drums series is intended to run alongside any external drum tuition methods and systems from video, book or a private teacher, so return here and to book 2 as soon as you are able to continue your growth.

GRAVITY Volume 1

Seriously, what does that mean? Why gravity and what does gravity have to do with drumming?

To answer that question, I will refer you to the Wikipedia description of gravity: Gravity, or gravitation, is a natural phenomenon by which all things with mass or energy — including planets, stars, galaxies, and even light — are brought toward (or gravitate toward) one another.

On Earth, gravity gives weight to physical objects, and the Moon's gravity causes the ocean tides. The gravitational attraction of the original gaseous matter present in the universe caused it to begin coalescing, forming stars – and for the stars to group together into galaxies – so gravity is responsible for many of the large-scale structures in the universe. Gravity has an infinite range, although its effects become increasingly weaker on farther objects.

So, we see that gravity really holds things together and on our planet earth, we experience gravity as a force that pushes objects of mass to the ground.

Whilst I had the idea to develop the Time Space and Drums Series, that thought was on my mind as I developed the first two parts of the series: Rock Drumming Foundation and Jazz Drumming Foundation.

Gravity forces mass and energy to the ground or nearest body so, because the first two books in the Time Space and Drums Series are foundational skills, I thought the analogy fit perfectly. Then there is the added bonus, if you like, that gravity also groups bodies together, drum beats if you will.

Closing Note:

The Time Space and Drums series is intended as a complete program from Part 1 to Part 12. It is strongly advised that you follow the program in order of the parts as they integrate and build on each other. The only thing I can now add is to practise each exercise until you have them all mastered. Mastery comes from paying attention to the most basic fundamentals already covered in each of the exercises within this book.

Once you have perfected each exercise, you may like to try them left-handed but that may take time, depending on your current skill level.

Free Audio Demonstrations

Please don't forget to visit the following URL to download audio demonstrations of every exercise in this book as soon as possible. You will then receive soma additional tips and guidance through the included essence emails.

www.timespaceanddrums.com/tsd-1pa.html

Your First Free Classified Document

Visit the following URL to download: In the Beginning - Creating A Universe
www.timespaceanddrums.com/p/beginning.html

What's Next

Thank you for choosing Time Space and Drums as one of your learning tools. I hope you enjoyed the process. You can explore more of the series in Gravity Volume Two, the second book in the series by searching for "**Jazz Drumming Foundation**" at your favorite bookstore.

Share Your Experience

If you have a moment, please review this Rock Drumming Foundation book at the store where you bought it. Help other drummers and tell them why you enjoyed the book or what could be improved. Thank you!

Thank you again dear reader and I hope we meet again between the pages of another book. Remember: You rock!

Other Books by The Author

Modern Drumming Concepts
Rock Drumming Foundation Series part. (Six in-depth Drum Lessons).
Jazz Drumming Foundation Series part. (Six in-depth Drum Lessons).
Rock Drumming Development Series part. (Six in-depth Drum Lessons).
Jazz Drumming Development Series part. (Six in-depth Drum Lessons).
Odd Time Drumming Foundation Series part. (Six in-depth Drum Lessons).
Accents and Phrasing Series part. (Four in-depth Drum Lessons).
Basic Latin Drumming Foundation Series part. (Four in-depth Drum Lessons).

Printed in Great Britain
by Amazon

84938559R00038